Federalism and European Union after Maastricht

Geoffrey Denton

January 1993

WILTON PARK PAPER 67

Report based on Wilton Park Conference 384: 6–10 July 1992: Federalism, 'Subsidiarity' and the European Community: How Can Common Decision-making be Combined with Democratic Control in the Community and its Member States?

LONDON: HMSO

ISBN 0 11 701752 3

ISSN 0953–8542

Contents

Foreword

Despite being planned twelve months earlier, this conference proved remarkably timely, since it took place approximately one month after the 'no' vote in the Danish referendum on the Maastricht Treaty had intensified an already vigorous debate about the future of the European Community. Federalism, regarded in some EC member states, such as Germany, as a normal constitutional structure, and in others, such as France and the United Kingdom, as an anathema that should not be discussed, became a concept at the heart of debate about the nature and future development of the Community. Subsidiarity, a term which had hardly reached the political consciousness of most of Europe before 1992, became a key slogan as politicians tried to re-assure concerned electorates that in giving greater powers to the European Community they would at the same time restrict the Community only to those competences that could not better be exercised at the national, or the regional level.

The structure of this conference also proved particularly apposite; including discussion of the federalist practice and experience of Germany and Switzerland, the centralising system and tendencies in France and the United Kingdom, and the difficulties of adaptation of member states with different constitutional and political experiences to a single European 'federal' model.

The theory and practice of federalism has been the subject of many books and learned articles. A working definition for our purposes would be: "The allocation of competences to the appropriate level of government". This concept poses no problems for countries such as Switzerland or Germany which have experience of operating federal systems. In some other member states, however, federalism is feared as either: a. centralisation of decision-making in Brussels, identified in particular with the EC Commission assuming excessive powers; or b. fragmentation of national sovereignty by enhancing the powers of the regions; or c. both centralisation upwards and fragmentation downwards. These fears are particularly marked in the United Kingdom, which although it has some regional devolution to Scotland,

Wales and Northern Ireland, has a long history of concentrating decision-taking at the national level in Westminster.

Until recently 'subsidiarity' was virtually unknown in Britain, and Wilton Park were criticised for putting the word into the title of this conference. In order to alleviate the fears of some member states of the loss of sovereignty to a (federal) union, the Maastricht Treaty, while omitting the word 'federal', incorporated the concept of 'subsidiarity'. For EC purposes, this means, briefly, introducing the safeguard that competences should be exercised at the lowest feasible level of government; or to put it another way, that the case for allocating competences to the centre has to be proved. However, such a simple definition requires to be developed by defining what the concept may mean in the particular circumstances of individual countries and of different aspects of policy in the European Community.

1 Federal Europe versus L'Europe des Patries

The European Community originated in two main objectives of the 'fathers' who had the task of rebuilding democratic Europe after the Second World War. The first was political: to prevent renewed conflict between European states, especially France and Germany. The second was to unify markets by removing barriers to trade, investment and labour movements so as to promote economic growth and prosperity. A strong linkage was perceived between economic integration and preventing conflict. To achieve these objectives, the Treaty of Rome created *sui generis* institutions: the Council of Ministers, the Commission, and the European Parliament. These institutions were and remain a mixture of the supranational and inter-governmental. The powers of the Commission to administer some common policies and to initiate new Community legislation are a form of surpranational power, as is the rather slight power of the European Parliament as co-decision-maker. But the decision-making powers of the Council are decisive for the development of the Community, and they remain inter-governmental.

The EC achieved its Customs Union, together with the Common Agricultural Policy, before the end of the 1960s. It failed to achieve by 1980 the economic and monetary union envisaged in the Werner Plan of 1970, but succeeded during the 1980s in establishing a remarkably successful European Monetary System (EMS), with its exchange rate mechanism (ERM) for stabilising exchange rates.

A decisive development of the Community's institutions came about in the Single Market Treaty of 1987, devoted to 'completing' by 1992 the removal of barriers to trade and competition across the internal borders. Supranational aspects of the Community were enhanced by acceptance of more majority voting and a greater role for the Commission in drafting almost 300 directives regulating many aspects of economic activity in the member states. In the light of later events it seems strange that this Treaty was supported most strongly by a United Kingdom Government which took a minimalist view about the role of government not only at national but especially at the EC level.

'Nationalists' and 'Federalists'

From the beginning of the 'European idea' there has been a continuing debate between supporters of the supranational and the inter-governmental approaches. Sometimes the debate has been open, in the sense that the choices were transparent; but in many cases debate was conducted at a technical level without apparent awareness among the protagonists that this fundamental matter of constitutional structure was at stake. Basically, the debate contrasts the positions of those who may be deemed 'nationalists' and those who may be called 'federalists'. (Using these labels is not meant to imply anything other than that these contrasting positions are taken on this particular issue.) Nationalists believe that a European union can be built on the basis of decisions taken by inter-governmental meetings such as those of the EC Council of Ministers, or at the heads of government level by the European Council. Federalists believe that to be effective a European union must be based on institutions endowed with supranational powers. The debate goes back at least to the period between the two World Wars. Following the Second World War the Congress of Europe held at The Hague in 1948 resolved in favour of a political, economic and cultural 'union'. However, governments were not willing to provide this union with supranational powers, and the outcome was the inter-governmental Council of Europe. Simultaneously, the supranational road was being followed with the establishment of the functional European Coal and Steel Community (ECSC), which established a High Authority to exercise powers in the coal and steel sectors of the six member states rather than relying on decision by periodic meetings of ministers. This supranational approach was widened in the Treaty of Rome, which established the European Economic Community (EEC) with substantial supranational powers: a permanent Commission to initiate as well as to implement legislation, and a Parliamentary Assembly. This line of development was blocked by the French in 1965, resulting in the 'Luxembourg Compromise' which effectively established consensus, that is national veto, as the basis for EEC decision-taking.

Paradoxically, further progress towards supranational decision-making had to wait for the Single European Act of 1987, an Act strongly supported by the British Government as a measure for freeing markets throughout the Community. In order to gain the economic advantages of free competition throughout the Single Market area, the British and other governments were willing to allow a substantial extension of majority voting: that is, a substantial reduction in their own power of veto over Community decisions. Meanwhile, supranational institutions had also been strengthened by the institution of direct elections to the European Parliament, and some additions to its powers of co-decision with the inter-governmental Council of Ministers.

Negotiations in the inter-governmental conferences (IGCs) on political union and on monetary union in 1990 and 1991 centred on the different positions of the member states on this central constitutional question. Although the United Kingdom and Denmark were characterised as the two states which held so strongly to the inter-governmental position that they could only be accommodated by special protocols, the other Ten member states were by no means unanimous and wholehearted in their support of a supranational solution. And if their governments were prepared to go along with the Treaty as it finally emerged at Maastricht, later events have shown that persuading parliaments and peoples to support evolution of the Community in the form agreed at Maastricht is by no means easy.

The Maastricht Treaty which emerged from the IGCs in 1991 was thus a hard-fought compromise between 'federalists' and 'nationalists'. It contained one decisive supranational development: the economic and monetary union to be completed by 1997 or possibly 1999. This would clearly require a common monetary policy managed by a European central bank; more controversially, it could require further constraints on the fiscal policies of member states. The Treaty also included aspects of political union but kept them largely of an inter-governmental character: a Common Foreign and Security Policy (CFSP), and an Internal Security Policy. The Social Charter was agreed separately by eleven member states, with the United Kingdom opting out.

The common assumption that the Maastricht Treaty would be duly ratified during 1992 and would come into force in January 1993 was challenged by the Danish rejection of the Treaty in a referendum on 2 June 1992 by a 0.7 per cent majority. This intensified the debate between 'federalists' and 'nationalists' throughout the European Community. Meanwhile, German opinion was expressing doubts of a rather different kind about the Maastricht Treaty, focused on fears that the strong DeutscheMark, deemed responsible for much of the success of German economic policy, would be lost in a weaker, more inflationary ECU currency area.

2   Federal Integration and Federal Devolution

Federalism is not one specific, well-defined system of government. Federalism refers to a spectrum of constitutional systems of which the US is the major, but by no means the only, historical example. These systems range from those which come close to a unitary state, as in the US, or Germany, to those which are only loose associations or 'leagues' designed to enable a number of still largely sovereign states to co-operate over a defined range of common interests. Examples of the latter include 16th century Netherlands and 20th century Western Europe.

Federalism is no Utopia, nor is it a panacea for avoiding conflict. Many wars have been fought by or within federations. The American civil war, fought to prevent the secession of a group of member states, is the most obvious example; the Nigerian civil war is a more recent example, and the Yugoslav civil war a current stark reminder. Unitary states may lead to tyranny, because of the opportunity they provide for a single individual or a small oligarchy to wield unrestrained centralised power. Federations have the advantage of dividing power, but suffer from a 'genetic' incentive to conflicts about the relative powers of the federal and the regional governments.

Federations are not uni-directional but have different modes in different circumstances. In some situations they can be forces for integration: in others, for decentralisation or even disintegration. The European Community, so far, has been an example of a 'federal' system in the integrating mode.

Federalism is a system adopted precisely in order to achieve a political compromise: between the benefits of interdependence and the benefits of separation; it combines union with autonomy. The union represented by a federation is more than an inter-national organisation, more than an alliance, more than even the closest of international relations, especially in that it is permanent and not temporary. By the same token, the autonomy enjoyed by constituent states within a federation must be less than total sovereignty.

States Rights

This gives rise to the crucial question about the rights of the component states within a federation. Constitutional theorists commonly agree that the federal government is greater than governments at the sub-federal level because there is no right of secession in a true federation. They assert that in a federation, autonomy confers three rights. First, there is the right of existence; the states have the right to continued existence which must not be curtailed by a federal government abolishing them. This is what distinguishes the states of a federation from regional or local government authorities in a centralised system, which may be created or abolished at the will of the central government. Secondly, the states in a federation have the right to act in specified areas, reserved to them under the federal constitution. The right to act in specified areas requires lists of powers or competences to be exercised at the different levels of government, and these lists can only be amended by agreement. Thirdly, the states have the right to participate in the federal (central) government, which requires a constitutional structure giving states powers to influence and co-determine policy with federal political organs. This right is normally effected through represen- tation of provinces in a second chamber, such as the German Bundesrat, with powers of veto over constitutional amendments.

Federalism itself implies the listing of competences and their allocation to the different levels of government. Subsidiarity adds the condition that in such allocation powers must be retained at the lowest feasible level. In many federal constitutions this principle is embodied in a constitutional clause reserving to the states all powers not explicitly endowed upon the federal government. The principle of subsidiarity can be used also to re- open discussion about competences already given to the federal level, which after due political debate could be re-assigned to the provinces.

The motives for forming federations are complex and not easy to define in theoretical terms; every actual federation appears *sui generis,* since each responds to a particular set of geographical and historical circumstances. A common motive is security, either against an external threat (for example, the stimulus given to the EC by the perceived threat from the Soviet Union) or against the internal threat of domination by one member, which may be

7

'contained' within a federation (Germany within the European Community?). A second major motive for federations is highly complex: a need to combine homogeneity with diversity. Federations require some degree of homogeneity in terms of sharing similar values; they are democratic systems; or if not, a federal structure will be spurious, as in the case of the Soviet Union's 'divide and rule' constitution. At the same time federalism implies a degree of diversity, without which a unitary state would be preferred. Common types of diversity, which lead to the federal solution when they co-exist with fundamental homogeneity, are ethnic, religious and linguistic differences, as evidenced in federal states as varied as Switzerland, Canada or the former Yugoslavia. In these cases a federal structure enabled the ethnic and other differences to be reconciled with political organisation to promote the security and welfare of the federation as a whole.

The institutional structures of federations, which give effect to some of these principles, are varied. The most famous, the US federal system, is based on a firm separation of powers, with a House of Representatives of the people, a Senate giving equal representation to each state within the federation, regardless of wide discrepancies in the size of their populations, and an executive President directly elected by the whole people. Whereas the US federation is one predicated on the presidential system of government, most European governments follow the parliamentary system. The German Bundesrat, therefore, is a chamber of governments, as is the Council of the European Community, whereas the US Senate is a chamber of individuals who need not represent the views of their state governments.

Federalism and Democracy

The different structures of federations and unitary states inevitably give rise to the question: which is more democratic? This question is not capable of any categorical answer. Federalism is more democratic than the unitary system of government in that power is divided. Indeed, a common judgement on the US constitution is that power is so divided as to reside nowhere: giving rise to an excess of democracy and an absence of efficiency.

On the other hand, by giving equal rights to all the states, however small, in a Bundesrat, Senate, or EC Council of Ministers, a federal system may allow decisions in certain circumstances to go against the expressed wishes of even a large majority of the people. This undemocratic feature of federalism has to be set against the benefits of mutual control exercised by the checks and balances in a system of divided powers.

Federalism is not so much a fixed constitutional arrangement as an ongoing process. A federal constitution may be determined quickly, as in the US Convention of 1787, or by a slower process of accretion of powers to the federal level, as in the EC since the 1957 Treaty of Rome, but there is usually provision for amendment, and the pressure of events over many years can give rise to substantial changes in the actual constitution and even more in the way it is interpreted and applied in practice. Federations are sometimes interpreted as systems of separate sovereign states on the way to complete union. However, in other examples there is evidence of federations moving away from the unitary end of the spectrum and back towards more autonomy for the member states. Supreme Courts or similar constitutional arrangements play an important role in interpreting the constitution and therefore in its development in either the integrating or the disintegrating direction.

A Right of Secession?

The most controversial element in this account of the theory of federalism is the right of secession. While countries may be willing to join a federal union of democratic states in order to gain the advantages of common action while retaining the benefits of autonomy, there is a natural tendency to cling to an ultimate national sovereignty on which to fall back if national interests appear not to be met by the institutions and policies of the federation. From this point of view a right of secession appears not only to be democratic, in the sense of being consistent with the fundamental right to self-determination, but also to be a necessary safeguard of the interests of the people.

Fear of the irreversibility of a federation may explain the public mood in the European Community after Maastricht; it is certainly exploited by opponents of the Treaty who play on this fear and raise the bogey of EC interference in the most trivial aspects of economic and social life. The civil war in former Yugoslavia is cited in support of the case for a right of secession to be put into the constitution of any federation; if such a right is not granted, it is argued, the inevitable consequence is civil war when one or more member states judge that the federation no longer serves their interests.

However, building a right of secession into a federal constitution means that the federation can be unscrambled at the whim of any one of the contracting parties. A federation with such a constitutional provision would lack credibility, for its own members and for other states; a federal system requires a degree of permanence and commitment.

The solution to this apparent impasse on the issue of secession is to appeal to the overwhelming advantages most federations will have for their members. On this view, the right of secession is more a theoretical than a real requirement, since the costs of leaving a federation will normally be far greater than the benefits, and even a member state which feels that the federation is having some negative effects will choose voluntarily to stay within it since the consequences of leaving will be unimaginable or unacceptable.

Many historical examples support this view. Almost no federation is free for long from the complaints of one or other member state. Demands for more autonomy, separation or complete independence are voiced, but in the great majority of cases the problems are overcome by a new compromise and the federation continues. Cases of complete breakdown, resulting in armed conflict as states assert their right to secede, are fortunately rare.

Representation of Minorities

An important argument in favour in the continuance of federations is that in the presence of ethnic and other diversity they provide a voice in a federal chamber for a state representing a national minority not only within the federation as a whole, but also in many of the constituent states of the federation. During the existence of Yugoslavia as a federal state, Croats in Bosnia had this advantage, as did Serbs in Croatia. The dissolution of a federation not only fails to solve the problem of ethnic minorities; it exacerbates it because national minorities in the constituent, now independent, states lose the protection previously provided by the rights and influence of 'their own' state in federal institutions.

The relevance of theoretical discussion to the case of the European Community is primarily that it pinpoints the essential issue: whether the EC member states are sufficiently homogeneous in terms of shared values and objectives as to be able to reconcile within a federal structure their diversity in terms of ethnicity, language, religion, culture and economic development. Unfortunately, the theory only poses the question; it does not answer it.

A further fundamental question raised by the theoretical discussion concerns the diversity of the internal constitutional structures of European states. Some are unitary, others federal; most are based on the parliamentary system, but one at least is more presidential. The question arises, can a federation itself be made up of both federal and unitary states; or must a federation impose upon its members homogenous constitutional structures? This question will be discussed after the examination of constitutional structures in different European states in section 3 below.

3 Unitary and Federal States in Europe

France and the United Kingdom as Centralised Nation States

France and the United Kingdom are centralised to a greater extent than other states in Europe, and in marked contrast with the federal structure of Germany. However, France and the UK are centralised in rather different ways. In France centralisation is a principle of government; France is 'one and indivisible', even including colonial territories in distant parts of the world, which are endowed with the status of *départements d'outre mer*. Centralisation is not without its critics, who complain of: 'apoplexy at the centre; paralysis at the extremes', but it is certainly deeply imbued in the French psyche.

In the UK centralisation is not ideological, which indeed is not surprising given that the UK is not a nation-state but a multi-national state made up of the English, Scottish, Welsh and (Northern) Irish nations. However, the English nation is preponderant in territory, population and wealth, and indeed UK centralisation can be interpreted as a reflection of the will of the English nation to dominate its smaller partners. Centralisation of the UK is expressed most categorically in the assertion of power by the Parliament at Westminster. The attachment to centralised government in the United Kingdom is explained in part by a long standing concern with the question of sovereignty. The concept of sharing power is alien to political philosophy in the UK, where political philosophers such as Hobbes and Dicey focused their reasoning around the question "Where does sovereignty lie?".

Despite the strong cultural centralisation of France, and its long *étatiste* traditions, in administrative practice France is not much more centralised than the UK; centralisation is more a legal form than a political reality. This point is evidenced by comparing the condition of local government in the two countries. In France local government has strong personalised leadership in the form of the Mayors who are elected chief executives with a great deal of independent power to manage their locality. The power and prestige of the Mayors is enhanced by the system of *'cumul des mandats'*, which allows for parallel political careers at the local and national, and indeed also at the EC, level. In the UK, by contrast, local government is largely separated from national government and a committee system introduced in an Act of 1835 prevents the emergence of strong executive leaders. Whereas 85 per cent of members of the French Assembly have local posts in addition to their membership of parliament, in Britain few politicians progress from local government to the national parliament. Local government is also represented in the French Senate, which has been described as *'le grand conseil des communes'*, and which indeed has some similarity to the second chamber in a federal constitution. This representation of subnational bodies at the centre was further strengthened with the introduction of regional authorities. Many members even of the French Cabinet are also Mayors.

In the United Kingdom the electoral systems allows one party to dominate particular areas of the country. Members of Parliament who have experience as local councillors usually become MP for a different area and so the link between the MP and the locality where he gained his political experience is broken. The House of Lords by no means fulfils the role *vis à vis* United Kingdom local government of the Senate in France.

Paradoxically, during the 1980s the UK became even more centralised, and in a more ideological way, whereas during the same decade France became more decentralised for pragmatic reasons. In the UK the lack of any constitutional constraint on the power of the Westminster government allowed the Prime Minister to abolish the Greater London Council and other authorities, handing over their powers to non-elected bodies. Controls were also imposed on the taxation powers of local authorities by the 'capping' of rates and later the Community Charge (Poll Tax). This left local authorities little role other than to implement central government policy where they are statutorily required to do so; they were left with little possibility of financing any discretionary policies of their own. At the same time, the central government moved away from consultation with local authorities on policy changes.

The UK tradition of asserting the sovereignty of Westminster explains the marked reluctance of the major political parties to embrace the concept of federalism, and therefore much of the opposition to development of the European Community in a federalist direction. The influence of 'Thatcherism' in the 1980s naturally reinforced this antagonism to federalism.

It is perhaps surprising, given these feelings, that the UK is prepared to share sovereignty in the North Atlantic Treaty Organisation, in such a vital area as defence, but not with the European Community in less vital areas. However, the determinedly inter-governmental nature of NATO is more attuned to UK political philosophy than is EC institution-building.

An interesting question raised by the Maastricht Treaty is whether the regional consultation committees established under it would require regional devolution of some kind in all member states in order that regions could be validly represented. Would the UK Government be entitled merely to nominate representatives for this committee, or would it, in order to comply with the Treaty, be required to allow that they should be appropriately elected or appointed by local authorities?

The Federal Republic of Germany

In marked contrast to the centralisation of the United Kingdom and France, the Basic Law of the Federal Republic of Germany, drafted in 1949 and owing much to the influence of the occupying powers in the three Western zones, has a federal structure. Article 28 of the Basic Law provides a federal guarantee of the Länder constitutions. The original eleven Länder of the Federal Republic before unification had great diversity in size, from the historic state of Bavaria and the massive Land Nordrhein-Westphalen to the city states of Hamburg and Bremen. Unification in 1990 added five eastern Länder to make a total of sixteen. The Länder elect their own parliaments, and the rights of counties (*kreise*) and communes (*gemeinden*) are similarly protected. Länder, counties and communes have the right to regulate their own affairs as they please subject only to the limits imposed by the Basic Law. The Länder also participate, under Article 50, in the legislation and administration of the federation as a whole through the upper house, the Bundesrat, consisting of members of the Land governments, which have the power to appoint and to recall them.

As in any federation, there are diverse views about the distribution of competences and the overall success of the constitution. In practice, Länder powers apply to the areas of education, local government, police and cultural activities. In addition to exercising their own powers in these areas, the Länder have a responsibility to execute federal law within their own territory. There are disputes among the Länder and between the Länder and the Federal Government especially in the area of education. The system of distribution of tax revenues among the Länder, *finanzausgleich,* is also a natural focus for controversy. An historic state such as Bavaria naturally tends to be more positive about the rights of the Länder than newly-created units which lack the same sense of historical identity. The principle of subsidiarity is not explicitly included in the Basic Law, although various Articles imply that this principle does in fact operate. In particular, Article 30 requires the exercise of governmental powers and the discharge of governmental functions by the Länder: "in so far as this Basic Law does not otherwise prescribe or permit".

This federal structure raises problems about ratification of the Maastricht Treaty, which would imply handing over to EC level some powers currently exercised by the Länder. Agreement of the Länder must be obtained before the Federal Government can ratify the Treaty, and there are proposals that a new revised Article 23 of the Basic Law may be needed so that the Länder may determine Germany's position on these matters at EC level.

Federal structures certainly create complications, and raise the question: how much diversity can be tolerated? If an EC federation is to develop, it will have to tolerate diversity as wide as that between a Federal Republic of Germany and the centralised nation states: France and the UK; and in future a Swiss Confederation with 25 independent cantons and a strong tradition of direct democracy.

The Swiss Confederation

Given the great ethnic and linguistic diversity of Europe, Switzerland has indeed often been regarded as a better model than Germany for a European federal state. It was no accident that the

1946 speech of Winston Churchill calling for a United States of Europe was delivered in Zürich, and it has been said that: "if Switzerland is a little Europe, the European Community is an enlarged Switzerland". However, the Swiss Confederation arose out of particular geographical and historical circumstances, and it is not easy to see how its structure could be used as a model for a federation on a completely different scale.

Switzerland was not originally multi-national; it started its 700-year history with a group of German-speaking cantons in 1291, and down to 1798 all the Swiss cantons were German-speaking with the exception of bilingual Fribourg. The purpose of the federation was not a closer union but defence from external threats. Swiss federalism therefore emphasised the autonomy of the cantons. Some cities and cantons were conquered before 1815, while others joined voluntarily. In this way four French-speaking and one Italian-speaking canton were added to 14 German-speaking and three multi-lingual cantons. Thus, Switzerland acquired three official languages, German, French and Italian; Romanche was recognised in 1938, but only as a national, not an official, language. To linguistic divisions are added religious distinctions, with a near equality in the number of Catholics and Protestants. Thus, every Swiss belongs to several groups at the same time and these multiple identities make the Confederation more stable than in federations which are split between two major groups, as for example in Canada or Belgium.

Stability is fostered by the rule that population movements are not allowed to change the language borders. The principle of 'territoriality' of languages means that the language(s), of a particular canton is (are) fixed; meanwhile, the principle of 'freedom' of languages gives the right to each citizen to be educated in his own language. In dual language cantons both languages must be taught in schools. In parliament and other national bodies, each member uses his own language and others are expected to understand. This rule works well with respect to German and French speakers; Italian speakers are disadvantaged because Italian is not widely understood in other parts of

Switzerland, and Italian speakers frequently find themselves obliged to use French or German in order to be understood.

In the seven-member Federal Council at least two members must be non-German-speaking; in practice three usually are French or Italian-speaking, thus giving a disproportionately high representation to the smaller language groups. Cantons similarly apply a principle of 'voluntary proportionality' which in effect provides disproportionately high representation for minorities within the canton. This highly tolerant procedure clearly plays an important role in ensuring peaceful acquiescence in minority status.

As in the US, the second chamber has two representatives from each canton, giving a similarly disproportionate representation to the small cantons, which are protected at the expense of a 'democratic deficit'. The system may be criticised not only for being undemocratic, but also for making decision-taking extremely complicated. In addition to the difficulty of obtaining decisions through standing representative bodies, provisions in the constitution for frequent resort to referenda have contributed to a deeply conservative polity in which evolution takes place with immense difficulty and at a snail's pace.

The hallmarks of the Swiss Confederation are direct democracy, federalism and neutrality. Membership of the EC, which was under consideration during 1992, but was implicitly rejected by a referendum decision in December 1992 against the European Economic Area (EEA), threatens to undermine all three principles; Switzerland, soon after its 700th anniversary, faces a massive challenge to its identity. Some even fear that its cohesion will be affected, with its component parts seeking to join the neighbouring states. Nevertheless, it is widely felt among the political elites that Switzerland has no alternative but to join the EC. It is already dependent on EC markets, and in common with other EFTA states Switzerland judged that the EEA did not meet its need to be involved in EC decision-taking. One of the major objectives of the Swiss Confederation in 1848 was to create a single economy, and the confederation for that reason was endowed with all the major powers over economic policy. Similar logic must now be applied in a world which has advanced far in terms of technology, transport and communications.

Assuming it can overcome the obstacles to accession, Switzerland will have problems in implementing EC legislation with which individual cantons may not agree. The Federal Government will have a right to impose such legislation under constitutional provisions allowing them to impose 'urgent' laws. However, one can envisage substantial clashes between the principle of the primacy of EC law and the Swiss tradition of direct democracy. Adaptation to EC membership is likely for this reason to be more difficult for Switzerland than for most other European states.

4 Widening and/or Deepening? EC Strategy at a Cross-roads

The question whether EC strategy should emphasise and prioritise 'deepening' or 'widening', or pursue both with equal urgency emerged with such great salience in 1992 because the EC must determine its future in the radically altered Europe of the 1990s. During the period of the perceived Soviet threat, the Cold War, the division of Germany and the occupation of Eastern Europe, the EC was subjected to substantial pressures leading it to concentrate on securing Western Europe and promoting its prosperity. In the new Europe it faces numerous new problems which meet with confused reponses. The removal of the Soviet threat has made integration appear to many no longer essential for European security. For others, the risk, and increasingly the fact, of turmoil and conflict in the East points to the opposite conclusion: that disintegration could spread from the East to de-stabilise the West, and must therefore be countered by rapid progress in strengthening the integration of Western Europe and simultaneously extending its contribution to political and economic stability by widening its membership, if only at the level of association.

Similarly, the implications of German unification are judged in diverse and contradictory ways. To some, unification, with its short-term de-stabilising effects on Germany and the EC but long-term promise of greater German power and prosperity, implies a greater urgency for integrating Germany more firmly into the Community. For others, it is a reason to fear German domination within the Community, and therefore to hold on to national sovereignty.

Debate about the internal development of the European Community ('deepening') has been accompanied by consideration of further enlargement ('widening'). The EFTA states negotiated between 1989 and 1991 the EEA in order to safeguard their access to the Common Market following implementation of the Single Market programme, but this device proved inadequate even before it had been concluded. First, their experience in negotiating the EEA led the EFTA states to judge that it was essential to be involved in EC decision-making if their interests were to be given due consideration. Secondly, with the collapse of the Soviet Union and the ending of the Cold War the maintenance of neutrality became a less essential security policy for Austria, Finland, Sweden and Switzerland. All these states have applied to join the EC, and Norway followed later in 1992. The states of East-Central and South-Eastern Europe also wish to join the Community at the earliest possible moment, for both economic and security reasons. In the Mediterranean, Turkey, Cyprus and Malta have already applied to join. Assuming that the Maastricht Treaty is ratified, the EC will be in a position to start negotiations with the EFTA states with a view to membership by January 1995. East-Central and South-Eastern Europe, and the Mediterranean states, raise more problems and may not be admitted to membership until around the year 2000 or even later.

Widening and deepening cannot be kept entirely separate. Some EC member states (the UK and Denmark) are keen to admit new members from Northern Europe because they believe these states would increase support for the looser inter-governmental development of the Community rather than the supranational evolution favoured by France and southern member states. By the same token, France and some other member states may prefer to defer widening until the Community has developed its structures and policies further. Beyond these tactical considerations, widening will in any event have substantial implications for the development of the Community. Institutions will have to be reformed to cope with 18 rather than 12 member states, and further reformed to cope with further increases in the number of members. Monetary union would not pose major problems for the stable and prosperous EFTA states, but could be more problematical for Eastern Europe. In the inter-governmental area of the CFSP, adding more member states will not make it easier to achieve the necessary unanimity on policy responses to crises, such as in Yugoslavia.

The need to widen the Community at the same time as it is deepening its policies suggests that the future structure of the EC will be highly complex and differentiated. While there may continue to be a central *acquis communautaire* which must be adopted by all new members, subject only to transitional arrangements, long-lasting or even permanent exemptions may have to be agreed for some of the policies included in the Maastricht Treaty. How to devise a structure coherent enough to give the Community effective direction while at the same time sufficiently differentiated to meet the individual needs of so many non-homogenous members is the great puzzle for the constitution-builders of Europe, whether of the 'federalist' or of the 'nationalist' persuasion.

The question of widening the Community also becomes intertwined with the choice between supranationalism and intergovernmentalism. Again, the arguments go both ways. Federalists argue that the Community can only meet the needs of existing and new members adequately if it is organised on a supranational basis with reformed institutions capable of coping with the greater complexity of more numberous members. Those who fear that widening means a looser structure give priority to deepening in order to 'secure' the Community before it faces the challenge of wider membership.

Supporters of the inter-governmental approach argue on the

contrary that enlargement of the Community will only reinforce the futility of attempting to make supranational methods work, and that with wider membership the Community must accept that only the inter-governmental approach is feasible. They want to give priority to widening in the expectation that it will head off attempts to enhance the powers of the Community's supra-national institutions.

Yet others persist in the judgement that the EC can and should deepen at the same time as it widens, because the Community has no option but to secure its internal structure and effectiveness while at the same time meeting the urgent demands for accession. They accept the need to persuade public opinion to support a Europe-wide federation, with unity for essential purposes combined with separate identities and decision-making powers to recognise the diversity of European nations and regions.

The prospects that such an advance on both fronts will be supported by the new members seeking accession to the EC appear doubtful. Some believe that small states have been among the strongest supporters of European union because it gives them a constitutional structure within which to form coalitions to counteract the dominance of big states. On this argument, the accession of more small member states should increase support for a federal structure. However, the accession of the EFTA countries could head-off deepening of the Community; it is suggested that their attachment to democracy, and their opposition to continental-style bureaucracy, will lead these states to side with Denmark and the United Kingdom against deepening and in favour of the Community as a looser free trade area and single market. Yet others believe it is impossible to generalise in this way about the position of the EFTA countries; they have so many different political parties and fluctuating public opinions such that it is impossible to predict which way their votes would go.

The impacts of successive enlargements of the Community to include the EFTA states, three states in the Mediterranean and numerous states in East-Central, South-Eastern and Eastern Europe, broadly speaking to the north, to the south and to the east, would be quite different and need to be discussed separately. The EFTA applicants have GDPs per capita above the EC average, and are therefore more readily assimilated than the much poorer states in the south and the east. As already noted, all the EFTA states are small in relation to the existing size distribution of EC members. The problem of super-small member states (SSMS) will be exacerbated not only by the accession of Iceland and Liechtenstein, which could possibly join with the other EFTA states in the mid 1990s, but also by Malta at a later date. There would then be pressure for some special arrangement to exclude these SSMS from all the rights of member states currently enjoyed by Luxembourg. This, however, could not well be done unless these rights were removed from Luxembourg, which would certainly fight vigorously to retain rights which it has enjoyed as one of the founder members of the Community since 1958.

More important than the number and size of the new states may be the question of the direction in which they will try to influence EC policy. The EFTA states are highly democratic, with powerful parliaments, ombudsmen, and traditions of respect for individual rights, open government and calling governments to account. They will increase the pressure for more openness in the development of Community policies, against decision-making in secret meetings of the Council of Ministers and in favour of more power to the European Parliament. Austria and Switzerland both have federal constitutions, and would reinforce Germany as member states who understand how federalism works, are not afraid of it, and indeed recognise its value for achieving unity for essential purposes combined with diversity elsewhere. The EFTA states also have strong traditions of direct democracy, including the use of referenda for decision-making, and this influence will further enhance the openness of debate on public policy, and accountability of governments at all levels to their electorates. Austria and Switzerland also have experience of how to run multi-ethnic communities; Switzerland has a still actual and very rich experience; Austria an historic tradition under the Empire and the Dual Monarchy.

If the EFTA states had already been members of the Community, the Maastricht Treaty would not have been drafted in the way it was, and many of the current problems about its ratification might have been avoided.

5 The Common Foreign and Security Policy

The development of a common foreign policy among the EC member states began informally in the mid-1970s with the process of 'European Political Co-operation' (EPC) conducted through inter-governmental meetings of EC member states organised outside the formal structure of the Community. Formal recognition of this process was provided in the Single Market Treaty of 1987. Under EPC, the EC member states' governments have gained valuable experience in consultations on foreign policy, and may have exercised some influence through their declarations of common policy positions on many areas of conflict, particularly the Middle East and Eastern Europe. The issue in the inter-governmental conference leading to the Maastricht Treaty was whether the common foreign policy should be given supranational authority by being conducted at least in part on the basis of majority voting, or whether it should remain a process of inter-governmental consultation with the right of veto for each member state. The second major issue was how far and in what way common foreign policy should be extended to common security policy or even to common defence. Underlying the answers to both these questions remained the long-standing issue of how far EC member states should co-ordinate their policies with the US, especially through NATO, or how far they should develop European institutions which could reduce the US role in Europe and US influence on the foreign policy of European states.

The answers to these questions as they resulted in the Maastricht Treaty were much nearer to the inter-governmental than to the supranational position. Implicit in the arguments between the supranational and the inter-governmental approach were the tensions between the large member states, who prefer the inter-governmental because it enables them to make informal agreements among themselves and to override the objections of the small states; and the small member states who mostly prefer the supranational method because it provides them with an opportunity to form coalitions and influence decisions taken in formal meetings by majority voting.

Some new procedures were included in the Treaty, including merging the EPC Secretariat with the Council Secretariat and stating that the Commission is "fully associated" with the policy. Thus, a small foreign policy unit within the Commission gives a slight supranational component in what remains primarily an inter-governmental procedure. The small member states wanted a role for the Commission, and an extension of qualified majority voting (QMV), since this would enable them to exercise some influence over the larger member states. This debate was mostly won by the large states, who insisted on unanimity for all the major decisions and would allow QMV only on matters of detailed implementation of policy.

The inclusion of security and even defence policy, together with a cryptic reference to a possible "common defence" appeared a major addition to the role of the Community as compared with EPC. However, given the continuance of national veto, it is hard to know what the practical implications of this part of the Treaty might be. Certainly, it opens the door for a substantial development of Community competence, and could become highly significant in the future if the member states so choose. Much will depend on how this part of the Treaty is interpreted and specifically on continuing discussions about the role of the different European institutions in security and defence.

First, it will be necessary to define the role of the Western European Union (WEU), which could have an enhanced role after Maastricht. It will also be necessary to continue the attempts to define how far WEU is to be a development of the European pillar *within* NATO, or how far it is to be the development of a European security and defence policy *independent of* NATO. This argument has continued over many years already, and the way it is handled in the Maastricht Treaty does not suggest that the debate will be brought to a conclusion in the near future. Secondly, it will be necessary to define how the Maastricht Treaty affects the role of the EC member states within NATO. Will they at some point in the future operate as a bloc with a single policy determined in their own council? Thirdly, it will be necessary to define what is the position of the EC with respect to the CSCE process.

An important aspect of the debate about security policy concerns the role of the Franco-German corps. This appears to have contradictory aims: partly to bring France closer to NATO, but at the same time to make NATO itself less relevant.

The future development of security policy in the Community will also be affected by Enlargement, and many questions remain to be answered also in this respect. Will new EC member states join the WEU? Will they be full members, or will they join only as associates or observers? Will some of the new EC member states even join NATO? How will the problem of traditional neutrality be handled?

The need for answers to some of these many questions which remain open is exemplified in the case of EC action towards events in the former Yugoslavia. The EC managed to operate a common foreign policy in several important respects: the establishment of a monitoring mission; the establishment of a peace conference under the chairmanship of Lord Carrington; the imposition of sanctions on Serbia; and joint recognition of three new states, Slovenia, Croatia and Bosnia. The importance of these elements of common policy should not be under-estimated. Any temptation to do so should be resisted by consideration of the consequences if these actions had not been taken in common but had been determined by individual member states acting on their own. The probability of tension and even dispute among EC member states, as individual states carried out policies not accepted by others, could have been most damaging to the political cohesion of the Community.

25

If the Maastricht Treaty had been in operation in time to be applied to the development of a CFSP in face of the events in former Yugoslavia, there could have been substantial advantages in the speed and effectiveness with which decisions were taken. However, on the biggest issue, recognition of the new states, a Maastricht Treaty providing for decisions only by unanimity would not have helped much. One difficulty was that Germany, the member state most keen to recognise the independence of Croatia and Slovenia, also has a Constitution forbidding any deployment of military forces outside its own territory. The German constitution needs to be changed, with the necessary two-thirds majority in the Bundestag, in order to allow Germany to participate in a CFSP which could determine, on occasions, the deployment of military forces outside the EC's territory.

The case of former Yugoslavia has also heightened the long-standing debate between reliance on the US and development of EC competences in foreign and security policy. Following the collapse and disintegration of the Soviet Union there was a general assumption that the EC would accept primary responsibility for policy in East-Central, South-Eastern and Eastern Europe; the US was certainly content to leave the EC in the prime role in reponse to the events in Yugoslavia. The relative ineffectiveness of the EC obliged the US to become involved itself, rather than leaving this problem, lying on their very doorstep, to be handled by the Europeans. Those, especially in the UK, the Netherlands and Germany, who have long supported the encouragement of a continuing US role in Europe are probably content with this outcome, but the debate continues.

Indeed, with regard to the CFSP the EC is a *'fédération malgré lui'*; others insist on regarding the EC as a power to be reckoned with, and the EC is obliged, however reluctantly, to attempt a common policy.

The potential applicants from East-Central Europe have no particular difficulty about the CFSP, since they are at least as ready to submerge their sovereignty in foreign policy, security and defence with the Community as are the existing member states.

The EFTA applicants, however, have long traditions of neutrality. While the EC had no formal CFSP, it appeared that they could join what was primarily an economic Community without any direct challenge to their neutrality. Indeed, the EC already contains one state, Ireland, with a foreign policy based on a kind of neutrality. But in applying for membership the EFTA states have to accept the *acquis* as it will be if the Maastricht Treaty is ratified and not only the *acquis* of the Treaty of Rome and the Single Market. They may well be in considerable doubt about what exactly this implies, but have to act on the assumption that the Community may develop a foreign policy based on majority voting, likewise a security policy, a defence policy, and even possibly a common defence. However, recent discussions of neutrality in the EFTA countries have tended towards the position that given the enormous changes in the global security scene since 1989, neutrality can no longer mean what it did during the Cold War and therefore will probably be abandoned quickly so long as there is no direct challenge to define its abandonment.

On the common assumption that the EFTA applicants will join the Community at an early date, possibly as soon as January 1995, the question arises whether the structure of the Community will change in such a way as to alter the approach to the CFSP, in the direction desired by small rather than large states. The existing Community of 12 has five large and seven small states. A Community of 18 with the addition of six EFTA countries (or 19 if Liechtenstein is included) would contain five large and 13 small states. Would the small states be able to prevail over the large? The common understanding in the large states is that they will continue to take the lead and to block any move to QMV even if they have difficulty in co-ordinating policy among themselves. The small states in fact face a dilemma. If they wish to see an effective EC policy they must want the large member states to work together; but if they do work together the small states will have little influence. If the small states are to have influence, they must press for QMV, but in political practice the large states are unlikely to allow themselves to be overruled when their national interests are seen to be at stake.

The conclusion on the CFSP is that the Community remains in a quandary. It faces external pressure to act as a single power; it recognises this and attempts to move in the direction of an effective CFSP; but since the larger states in particular, and on some issues also the smaller, are unwilling to abandon their sovereignty when important issues are at stake, they are not prepared to structure the CFSP so that it can be effective. The Maastricht Treaty summarised this quandary, and used language suggesting that there was potential for some movement towards an effective CFSP, but without putting in place any convincing structures for achieving it. The British Foreign Secretary stated that his Government could not accept a CFSP which could by a majority vote determine policies putting at risk the lives of British Troops. Until the governments of member states are willing to accept such voting, it will not be possible to operate a common defence and probably not a coherent and effective CFSP.

6 The Debate on Monetary Union

The centre-piece of the Maastricht Treaty is the programme for creating a monetary union by 1997, or 1999 at the latest. With unification of the currencies and central control over monetary policy by a European central bank, this was the federalist, supranational part of the Treaty.

As is usual in monetary affairs, the debate on European Monetary Union (EMU) has been fast and furious in the months before Maastricht and since. Just as the Danish 'no' vote and the uncertainty about the French vote in the referenda on Maastricht raised the temperature on the political side, pressure mounted on the technical monetary issues. The strength of the DeutscheMark (DM) was enhanced by the high interest rates needed to counter the expansionary consequences of a public sector deficit amounting to 7 per cent of GDP to finance support for the eastern Länder. Additional pressures were created by the weakness of the US Dollar, which by September 1992 had fallen to DM 1.40 and £0.50.

As on previous occasions of Dollar weakness, the effect was to increase upward pressure on the DM. This occurred against the background of recession in other European economies. Calls for a re-alignment of the DM within the Exchange Rate Mechanism (ERM), and failing that re-alignment downwards of the central rate of the Lira, Sterling, and possibly other weak currencies, were accompanied by protests that moving to monetary union according to the programme laid down at Maastricht could have disastrous consequences in future by preventing similar necessary exchange rate adjustments.

Finally, the Italian Lira and the British Pound were forced out of the ERM in mid-September 1992. This was a massive blow to the credibility of the timetable for moving to stages 2 and 3 of monetary union laid down in a still unratified Maastricht Treaty. The French vote by a narrow majority on 20 September in favour of ratification hardly served to remove the political uncertainties that had helped to undermine the stability of the exchange rates.

The Maastricht Agreement on EMU assumed that there was already in place an effective monetary union centred on the ERM intervention system and its rules for the bilateral relationships of the member currencies: in practice a DM zone with the German Bundesbank setting its monetary policy and other member states falling into line. This system had worked remarkably well, with no currency re-alignments after 1987, even if at the cost of slower growth and higher unemployment in those countries which had to maintain an over-restrictive monetary policy in order to keep their currency within the permitted bands. The existence of the system meant that blame for the costs of monetary discipline could be laid on the Community, rather than on member state governments and central banks. However, policy constraints would have obliged the member states in question to maintain a strict monetary discipline even outside the exchange rate mechanism. For example, the fact that the UK was not in the ERM until October 1990 did not make the UK authorities feel free to adopt an independent monetary stance. On the contrary, they felt obliged on numerous occasions to keep in line with German monetary policy, with changes in UK interest rates following DM interest rate changes within hours.

EMU was intended to make the pseudo-monetary union already created by the EMS irreversible by abolishing the separate currencies and handing over management of monetary policy to a European central bank. This would have the advantage, over the EMS, of reducing uncertainty about the value of currencies to zero, thus removing the need for interest rate differentials which in effect are premia to encourage the holding of currencies whose value remains in doubt. It would also have the advantage that the European central bank would have a remit to serve the interests of the whole Community, thus removing the problem, in the ERM, that the Bundesbank's duty is to the Federal Republic, while the impact of its policy decisions on the other members of the system can be just as onerous.

Abolition of the national currencies would also bring the advantage of the elimination of transactions' costs. Whether this advantage is substantial or trivial is controversial; some claim that the charges made by the financial institutions for foreign exchange transactions are only a minor irritant and an insignificant cost of doing business across European frontiers, though firms and individuals appear to find these costs substantial enough to be worth eliminating. More important, but much harder to measure, is the cost of the remaining degrees of uncertainty about exchange rates, which inhibit cross-frontier investments and trading, and will persist until the EMS is made irreversible by conversion into an EMU.

The Criteria for EMU

The debate about EMU can be conducted on the basis of a number of deceptively simple questions: is EMU economically feasible?; is EMU economically desirable?; will EMU increase the rate of inflation?; will EMU raise the average level of unemployment?; is EMU possible without political union?; is political union feasible and desirable?

EMU is certainly feasible as articulated in the Maastricht Treaty, on the assumption that member states are able to comply with the criteria for joining. According to the Treaty, if it is ratified, EMU will come into effect in 1997 or if that fails, at the latest in 1999. In order to join the Union member states have to fulfil five criteria: to have inflation not more than 1½ per cent above the average of the three lowest inflation members; to have a long-term rate of interest not more than 2 per cent higher than that in the three lowest inflation members; not to have re-aligned their exchange rate during the previous two years; to have a general government borrowing requirement not greater than 3 per cent of Gross Domestic Product; and to have a ratio of public debt not more than 60 per cent of GDP.

Before September 1992 it seemed there would be little problem about fulfilling the first three criteria. Rates of inflation and of interest had already converged under pressure from the ERM rules, which had already helped to avoid exchange rate adjustments for five years since 1987.

With the floating and depreciation of the Lira and Sterling, and a devaluation of the Peseta, Italy, the UK and Spain have to recreate a credible stability in their exchange rates with the DM and the other ERM currencies. Their ability to do so will depend upon their success in exploiting the depreciation of their currencies to improve their real economic performance while holding in check the inflationary pressures deriving from higher import prices. Failure would lead to inflation and further currency depreciation and destroy any possibility of an EMU of all the EC member states before the next millennium. Success would mean that these countries could rejoin the long hard road back to credibility as partners in the EMU.

The problematical Maastricht requirements for the start of the EMU are those concerning the borrowing requirement and the level of accumulated debt. These requirements appear likely to be treated with some flexibility, as bench-marks rather than as categorical targets. They will probably be interpreted as standards towards which states should be making satisfactory progress. Nevertheless, in mid-1992 Germany itself was not in a condition to qualify; indeed, only France and Luxembourg would have qualified if these tests had been applied in 1992. Fulfilment of the criteria by 1997 or 1999 will require substantial improvement in budgetary performance on the part of Italy and Spain. The budgetary effects of its prolonged recession pushed the UK also into the group of non-qualifying countries. The smaller countries, Ireland, Portugal and especially Greece, may also have great difficulty in meeting these conditions.

A number of important secondary questions remain to be answered. What will happen to Dollar reserves? How will monetary policy be formed? How will the profits from the issue of ECUs be shared out? How will central banks comply with the rule of not bailing-out governments? How will central banks supervise their commercial banking systems? However, these questions are capable of being resolved without great difficulty.

Is EMU Viable?

On the fundamental question, whether the EMU is economically viable, economists have a wide range of opinions. The key issue is what will happen to inflation under EMU in comparison with the experience of the ERM. Over the whole period 1972-92, during which the Snake and then the EMS have operated, DM inflation has averaged about 5 per cent, which is not an adequate performance, though this 20 year period did include the two 'oil-shocks' of 1973-74 and 1980-81 and the 'unification shock' of 1990-92. It is argued that the European central bank will have a worse performance because the result of monetary union will be to have monetary policy determined not by the independent Bundesbank but by the non-independent central banks of EC member states with weaker currencies and less political determination to maintain price stability. On the other side of the debate, reference is made to the 13-year experience of the EMS before the crisis of September 1992, during which there was a gradual conversion of successive member states to monetary discipline, most notably that of the Socialist Government of France, which decided in 1983 to abandon its initial policy of growth-in-one-country and accepted the need to tie the Franc to the DM.

The fact that several EMS members had succeeded, albeit with some sacrifices, in squeezing out inflation and increasing the credibility of their exchange rate stability to the point where the differentials in interest rates had become very small, suggested that the necessary adjustments had already been made. With or without a move to EMU, these governments would be most reluctant to abandon the policy and revert to currency devaluation or depreciation, which could provide only a short-term boost to growth and employment, and at the expense of higher inflation and renewed economic problems later.

Underlying this discussion is the question whether real wages are flexible, and whether variable exchange rates are valuable as a means of adjusting them in the face of differentiated shocks affecting different member states unequally. The case of German unification is quoted as an example of the consequences of monetary union; monetary union in September 1990 was followed by massive falls in output and employment in 1991 and 1992. But this was an extreme case, since the conversion of Ost-Marks into D-Marks on a one-to-one basis (decided on political reasons rather than on the basis of economic calculation) brought about a sudden convergence of real wages. Some similarity is suggested between this case and that of a wider European monetary union, since abolition of national currencies and the denomination of wages in ECUs would create greater transparency and comparability of costs and prices across frontiers, and therefore exercise some pressure for real wage convergence. While this suggestion must be a matter for judgement based on detailed examination of labour market behaviour in the different economies, it would appear *ab initio* to exaggerate both the potential for real wage convergence in an EMU, and the possibilities for real wage variability with flexible nominal exchange rates.

In very large economies, such as the US and Japan, the dependence on foreign trade may be low enough for devaluation to adjust real wages without triggering inflation. In smaller economies such as those of the EC member states, trade interdependence is much greater, so that any real wage effect of currency depreciation/ devaluation may be eroded by compensatory increases in wages and other incomes. The matter can only be resolved by detailed study of the effects of parity changes in economies of different sizes and structures. It is widely agreed that the smaller EMS member states (Netherlands, Belgium, Luxembourg, Denmark, Ireland, Portugal) have little option but to maintain their parity with the DM, if they can. The case is not quite so clear for the larger EC economies. However, interdependence of their economies has been growing rapidly with the removal of barriers to trade in goods and services, and the abolition of controls on the movement of capital. Further increase of interdependence as the effects of the Single Market take effect will further strengthen the case for currency stability and therefore for EMU.

The benefit of adjustment in any one country is conditional on other countries not matching exchange rate depreciation in one country in an attempt to maintain their competitiveness. By definition, depreciation in one country means relative appreciation in another. In this case, parity changes are a beggar-my-neighbour policy which can only succeed for one country and only over a short period. While they can buy time within which structural adjustments (diversion of resources from domestic demand to exports) can in principle be made, they also remove the pressure to carry out those adjustments. Thus, all too often depreciation/devaluation allows a crisis in a country's external accounts, a symptom of lack of competitiveness, to be evaded rather than confronted.

The speculative pressure for revaluation of the DM pointed to a need for EMS re-alignment, effectively a relative devaluation of other EMS currencies against the DM. Such an agreed re-alignment could have prevented the exchange market crisis of mid-September 1992 which forced the Lira and the Pound out of the exchange rate mechanism. With benefit of hindsight, failure to re-align parities within the ERM, clinging to the pseudo-MU in the face of market signals that the existing parities were untenable, was a damaging failure of policy co-ordination among the EMS central banks and governments.

For some, this traumatic episode shows the folly of fixing exchange rates. They argue that this policy allows the Bundesbank to suppress growth in less competitive economies by a too rigorous monetary discipline; that is, that the ERM is fundamentally deflationary, slowing growth and raising unemployment in other EC economies; and that the EMU would be just as deflationary and with no possibility of escape. This argument, however, ignores the origins of DM strength in 1992 in the tight monetary policy conducted by the Bundesbank following the fiscal expansion in Germany needed to fund massive spending in the eastern Länder without raising taxes. Fiscal expansion boosted aggregate demand in the Germany economy and increased its rate of inflation. Given the interdependence of the European economies, Germany therefore stimulated output in other EC member states in 1990-92, and the tight monetary policy was a necessary adjustment. Those who 'blame' the Bundesbank for creating high real interest rates throughout Europe ignore the initial stimulus to demand given by German fiscal policy, and also the continuing high average level of inflation within the Community.

If real wages really are flexible following a change in the nominal exchange rate, then they should be flexible following wage settlements which while nominally positive fail to match continuing high rates of inflation. Only when inflation has been reduced near to zero will it be possible to argue that the ERM (or a future EMU) is operating in a deflationary way.

These arguments for devaluation are all too familiar, and usually proliferate during recessions. The recession of the early 1990s has not been particularly deep so far, but has been prolonged in the UK on account of debt overhang and declining asset values resulting from excessive expansion during the 1980s boom. This was prolonged by measures, taken after the Wall Street crash of October 1987, which although supported at the time by governments around the world proved in retrospect to have been mistaken. Once the world economy begins to pull out of the recession these arguments for flexible parities will fade away. The unfortunate conjuncture of the Maastricht Treaty and the debate about its ratification with recession in the European and world economies explains much of European events and politics during 1992.

The Social Chapter and EMU

The UK Government opted out of one aspect of the Maastricht Treaty, the Social Chapter, leaving the rest to a separate agreement. There are complex issues about the desirability of minimum working conditions as a means of promoting social responsibility and cohesion, and a significant difference of approach between the Anglo-Saxon economies and the continental European Christian Democratic tradition. The UK decision reflected this different approach to issues of minimum wages and working conditions and unwillingness to accept interference from Brussels in labour market matters.

There is also, however, an important question about economic strategy in a monetary union. If parity changes are not to be used as a means of economic adjustment, it will be all the more important to maintain flexibility in real wages and working conditions. Imposing minimum standards on all member states would interfere with the competitiveness of the weaker countries.

EMU and Political Union

Critics and supporters of EMU alike tend to agree that EMU must be accompanied by at least some aspects of political union. Reluctant or doubtful supporters of EMU may accept such a political union as a necessity, while enthusiasts for European integration regard it as desirable in its own right for political and security reasons, and therefore in itself an additional argument in favour of the EMU that will help to bring it about. Those who reject EMU tend also to reject political union, and those who are lukewarm about EMU often argue that it is the political implications that are particularly objectionable.

The Gold Standard, like the exchange rate mechanism, was optional; any country could decide to leave it at any time. By abolishing the separate national currencies and centralising monetary policy in a Eurofed, EMU will interfere more deeply with national sovereignty and is more irreversible. Political union is needed not only to provide a constitution and an ultimate political authority within which the Eurofed can exercise its competences; it is also needed to complement the common monetary policy by organising some common control over the fiscal stance of member states, in order to avoid the 'free-rider' problem of member states selfishly and irresponsibly attempting to offset the effects of EMU monetary discipline on their economies by indulging in fiscal expansion at the expense of other member states.

Finally, the EMU is contested on the ground that economic management is more successfully conducted and results in better economic performance in small than in big states. Mancur Olsen has referred to the 'distributional coalitions' which in large societies such as the US take up energy and reduce enterprise by devoting their efforts to securing a larger share in the national product rather than to increasing the national product. According to this argument, the US would have benefited from maintaining separate currency areas in its different regions, and the EC should avoid going down the road the Americans followed after the establishment of the Federal Reserve System in 1914.

Those who object to the political aspects of EMU neglect the fact that the EMS was itself the result of substantial political debate and decision-making. Political acts were needed to establish the European currency Snake in 1972, the EMS in 1979, the French acceptance of the discipline of the ERM in 1983 and UK membership of the EC in 1990. The political commitment needed to take these important steps towards convergence will probably seem in retrospect at least as hard as that required to take the final step of creating the EMU, which by making the process irreversible will make the fixed exchange rates more credible, the interest rate differentials lower, and will much reduce political contention.

Fiscal Policies in a Monetary Union

By its proposal for EMU by 1997 or 1999, the Maastricht Treaty raises more urgently than before issues about the EC budget and national finances that have long been the subject of debate. The EC budget started with member state contributions based on crude percentages of the total spending. The Community's 'own resources' were developed in the 1960s and 1970s in the form of customs duties, import levies and a share in national VAT receipts. However, further financing demands in the 1980s were met by reversion to member state contributions related to Gross Domestic Products. EC financing problems have been aggravated by the reluctance of member states to give the Community its own fiscal resources. Direct powers of taxation in the hands of the Community itself would make it more accountable as to how funds are spent. The EC budget is one area among many in the Community where the reluctance of member states to hand over decisions to Community level gives rise to problems that could be solved by applying sound principles of allocation of competences. In 1975 The EC Commission's MacDougall Report, triggered by the Werner Plan for economic and monetary union by 1980, attempted to clarify what kind of budgetary developments would be needed on various assumptions about the competences to be exercised at the Community level, especially the budgetary implications of monetary union. At the very least, the Report concluded, the EC would need a budget of about 2½ per cent of Community GDP. With the allocation of more competences to the Community level the budget would need to rise to about 5 per cent, or including defence, to about 7½ per cent of CGNP. On even more *communautaire* assumptions an EC budget of about 10 per cent of CGDP could be envisaged. This would still be small compared with the US federal budget of about 25 per cent of US GNP.

In the light of this report from the 1970s, proposals for the 1990s appear extremely modest with regard to the size of the 'optimally centralised' budget structure. The proposal in the 'Delors II' budget package, whose acceptance is regarded as one of the conditions for proceeding with the plans for MU, but which met considerable resistance from some member states, was to raise the EC budget ceiling from 1.2 per cent of CGDP to 1.37 per cent. On the assumption that with some competences passed to Community level member states could reduce their own budgets this increase should not pose any great problem. However, such decisions have always been politically contentious.

Sensitivity to any increases in the EC budget has been fostered by the concentration of its expenditures on the Common Agricultural Policy (CAP), which still takes almost 60 per cent of the total. From the stand-point of the principles of public finance, one of the greatest problems has been the irresponsibility of CAP decisions taken by agriculture ministers meeting separately from their finance ministers. Agriculture ministers have usually decided on target and intervention prices and have then in effect submitted the bill for the resulting subsidies, however high it might be, to the finance ministers. Even worse, the CAP's principle of Community 'solidarity' means that in making decisions even at the finance minister level, every country has an incentive to behave irresponsibly, since common financing spreads the burden of taxation among other member states.

The small size of the proposed Community budget raises the question whether it will be large enough to carry out adequate transfers from richer to poorer member states, and from richer to poorer regions of the Community, believed by many to be essential compensations for accepting the discipline of monetary union. Even a small budget can be 'highly geared', that is, structured to have a high proportionate redistributive element. The EC budget does indeed have a redistributive element, but given the way it has developed, not always in the progressive direction demanded by the poorer member states. Indeed, a perceived inequitable, regressive distribution of transfers has been a major issue in Britain's relations with the Community. The problem was resolved by agreement on 'abatements' to reduce the UK's net contribution to the EC budget, but the issue remains, and not only for the UK, and is revived whenever there is discussion of expansion of the budget.

Even if a will exists to assist the weaker EC economies to converge on the stronger economies, political constraints on the size of the EC budget, on its structure, and on the degree of gearing, mean that transfers are unlikely to satisfy the demands of the poorer member states.

But what exactly do they need? The key issue is whether wages will be equalised throughout an EMU, thus reducing the competitiveness of national economies with lower productivity. The case of German monetary union in 1990 following unification of the GDR with the Federal Republic has been cited above as an example of the problem. The German monetary unification, however, is not at all a model for EC monetary union. There will be no decision on any 1:1 basis for unifying DMs with Escudos! Further adjustment of parities may well take place following those of autumn 1992 before monetary union later in the decade. Monetary union will be on the basis of parities that reflect relative competitiveness of the economies at the moment of union. Any wage equalisation effects of MU will therefore be much weaker and much slower than in the case of Germany, as denomination of incomes in ECUs throughout the EC raises the transparency of differentials. The weaker economies will continue to compete, as they do at present, on the basis of lower real incomes than those in the richer member states. Workers, and their trade unions, have lived for many years with the knowledge that incomes are higher in some EC member states than in others; German civil servants and motor industry workers are better paid than British. Monetary union will not decisively increase knowledge of these differences, nor the use made of it.

Thus, while adjustment of monetary union may usefully be lubricated by some further fiscal transfers, embodied in a Cohesion Fund to be added to the existing Regional and Social Funds, fiscal transfers on the scale applying within Germany are not in question for the Community as a whole.

EC Constraints on Member States' Budgets

The Community will need to exercise some control over the fiscal structure of the member states so as to avoid the common monetary policy being jeopardised by irresponsible fiscal behaviour at the national level, equivalent at Community level to the controls existing at the national level over the fiscal decisions of regional and local authorities. Decisions by lower level authorities to finance spending out of borrowing rather than out of taxation could frustrate the policies of the Eurofed for the level of overall borrowing and of interest rates throughout the Community. If the optimum policy mix of monetary and fiscal measures is to be achieved, some control is essential. Ideally, this should be self-control on the part of member state authorities, but their decisions would have to be made in accordance with guidelines set at Community level.

This would not mean that each member state should maintain its budget at precisely the same percentage of national GDP as all other member states. Individual states could decide to have larger budgets if they were willing to finance additional spending out of higher taxes, and could design these taxes in such a way that they did not distort the conditions of competition within the Single Market. The scope for national variations in VAT and exise duties is being reduced with the abolition of fiscal frontiers in the Single Market from January 1993, which has obliged member states to accept a minimum VAT rate. This will narrow the range of fiscal independence left with the member states to direct taxes on incomes and capital. If they choose to raise these taxes in order to finance higher spending on social transfers and other social spending which did not improve competitiveness, member states could find their competitiveness in Community markets being eroded, putting pressure on them to adjust their spending and taxing towards the Community average. However, if higher spending were devoted to investments in education, training, research and infrastructure, which contributed to a higher level of competitiveness, there is no reason why a member state should not maintain over long periods higher levels of taxing and spending than other member states. This would be quite consistent with the operation of fiscal federalism.

Summary

1. There is a marked differentiation of constitutional structures in Western Europe, between France and the United Kingdom, which have a long tradition of centralised power, and Germany with a recent federal constitution, or Switzerland with a much longer federal history.

2.   While a federal constitution for a future European union appears a natural extension of the national constitution for Germany, it alarms many in other EC members states, especially in the UK, who fear a loss of national sovereignty both upwards to Brussels and downwards to regions.

3.   A constant theme in the history of federations is a struggle for power between the federal government and the states, evident from the time of their constituent assemblies or conventions. A compromise is usually embodied in federal constitutions or later amendments in the form of articles protecting 'states rights'. A key issue, that has led to much struggle and civil wars in the US in the 1860s, in Nigeria in the 1960s, and in Yugoslavia in the 1990s, is the right of secession.

4.   From the beginning of the 'European idea' there has been a keen debate between 'nationalists' who preferred an inter-governmental approach to integration, and 'federalists' who pressed for supra-national institutions. Those 'federalists' who emphasised the need to distribute power downwards also proposed a 'Europe of Regions', giving regions direct access to the federal institutions, and thereby implying even further reduction of national sovereignty.

5.   The inter-governmental conferences of 1990 and 1991, organised to determine the EC's response to new challenges posed by the collapse of Soviet power in the East, the unification of Germany and demands for accession by numerous countries in Northern, Eastern and Southern Europe, were contentious on how to adapt the Community, and most markedly along the 'nationalist' – 'federalist' divide.

6.   The compromise agreed in the Maastricht Treaty in December 1991 contained two major advances in European integration: an Economic and Monetary Union (EMU) by 1997, or 1999; and a less concrete but potentially significant Common Foreign and Security Policy (CFSP) including even a 'common defence'; plus common internal and border security

policies, and a 'Social Chapter', though the UK and Denmark secured 'opt-out' clauses. Only the EMU was supra-national, and that was conditional. The CFSP was firmly inter-governmental.

7. Despite keen public debates in the run-up to Maastricht, and the many compromises it embodied, the Treaty proved unpopular; it was narrowly rejected in June 1992 in a referendum in Denmark, and only narrowly approved in a French referendum in September; a final decision in the UK Parliament, and a second attempt to obtain ratification in Denmark, were deferred until well into 1993.

8. Meanwhile, the prospects for achieving its central objective of EMU were set back by crises in the Exchange Rate Mechanism (ERM); by the end of 1992 the UK and Italy had left the system, other members had been forced to devalue, and the assumption of a smooth progression from a stable ERM pseudo monetary union to a single currency had been destroyed.

9. Many technical issues complicate decisions on how to move forward on EMU. Eurosceptics argue that the events of 1992 have shown the futility of trying to unify the currencies of EC member states that still need the flexibility in national economic policy derived from parity changes. Others stress the beggar-my-neighbour character of competitive devaluations, the inflationary consequences of rising import prices, and the negative impact on trade and investment flows of unstable parities and economic policies.

10. The German Bundesbank was much criticised for creating problems for other states by single-mindedly maintaining its constitutional objective: price stability in Germany. There was certainly a failure of policy co-ordination among the EMS members. Two reactions are possible following these events: either to abandon the prospect of EMU and the existing EMS; or to replace the Bundesbank's dominant role in European monetary policy by subsuming it with the other

national central banks in a European Central Bank constitutionally required to promote the economic health of the Community as a whole.

11. Events also conspired to put the CFSP to the test before the Treaty could be ratified. The former Yugoslavia posed a dilemma to the EC whether to recognise Croatia and Slovenia, and later Bosnia, as independent states. European political co-operation functioned just well enough to prevent the disaster of different EC member states taking different positions, but the embryo CFSP was not capable of giving the decisive signals needed to prevent Yugoslavia sliding into inter-ethnic war, first in Croatia in 1991, then in Bosnia in 1992. The EC failed to live up to the expectations of neighbouring states that it should act as a great power.

12. Together with the overwhelming challenges to its core policies, EMU and CFSP, the EC also has to face up to demands for accession from the EFTA states, and later from Central, Eastern and Southern Europe. Although the EFTA states present relatively little problem for EMU or for CFSP, their accession will require adaptation of EC structures and decision-making. Whether they will strengthen the inter-governmental or the supra-national tendency, the 'nationalists' or the 'federalists', is not easy to predict.

13. After a tempestuous 1992, the EC faces a hard task in 1993 to define its identity and purposes and to recover its momentum. The future not only of the Community itself, but of the whole of Europe lies in the balance. The Wilton Park conference participants in the majority supported the case for 'federalist' solutions to economic, security and constitutional issues, an early move to EMU, a CFSP with more decision-making by majority vote, early enlargement, and significant reform of EC institutions in the federalist direction.

Conclusion

The Wilton Park conference participants, however, were well aware that they were not a representative cross-section of European public opinion. The public mood certainly had swung sharply towards a sceptical view about the European Community by the end of 1992, dashing the hopes and expectations of those who believed that a more deeply integrated, and a much wider, EC would be an important building block of a 'new world order' of peace and prosperity after the end of the Cold War.

Following the doldrums of the mid-1980s, the momentum of integration had appeared to be firmly established by the success of the Single Market '1992' Programme, and the great attraction of the Community, as a haven of political democracy and liberal market economies, to the emerging former Communist states of Central, South-Eastern and Eastern Europe. The stability of the EMS parities after 1987 appeared to reflect growing convergence, coherence and co-operation of the EC economies. The successes of EPC appeared a good preparation for a more ambitious CFSP, to organise a larger independent role for European foreign, security and even defence policy, as the diminution of the Soviet threat enabled the US to scale-down its commitments in Europe. Above all, a unified Germany wanted to be anchored firmly inside a federal Europe and other member states recognised the importance of building the new European order on this crucial strengthening of political and economic integration.

The events of 1992, which for many besides Queen Elizabeth II will be remembered as an 'annus horibilis', have shaken confidence in this hopeful scenario. A major cause of the difficulties has been the unfortunate coincidence of a prolonged and deep recession, in the US, in Japan, in the UK and in continental Europe (itself a consequence of the over-expansion in the 1980s boom) with the collapse of the Soviet and other socialist economies (brought about by sudden adjustment after decades of economic mismanagement). Some mistakes in handling the economics of German unification also contributed to the economic crises. Another cause was the too early challenge of the ethnic wars in former Yugoslavia to a not-yet-complete CFSP.

A mood of narrow-minded and short-sighted nationalism has caught hold, not only, as one would expect, among the unemployed and others suffering in the recession, but also among governing elites who adopt a 'suave qui peut' approach as they try to survive from one day to the next, as less scrupulous politicians make political capital out of the grievances of those who are suffering.

At the beginning of 1993 a renewed effort is needed to put European integration back on course, to restore stability to the EC economies, to lead Eastern Europe out of its savage adjustment into steady economic growth, and above all to give an example of political integration as the means of avoiding inter-national and inter-ethnic strife. A vital first step is to conclude ratification of the Maastricht Treaty, as a symbol of the determination of EC governments and peoples to work together and not to pull apart.

List of Participants

ALIAGAS, Spyros: Ministry of Foreign Affairs, Athens
ALLDEN, Hans: Riksdagen, Stockholm
ANGEHRN, Hans: Kantonschule of Sargans, St Gallen
ANTONSEN, Charlotte: Liberal Member of the Danish Parliament
ASDAHL, Lilian: Kantonschule, Heerbrugg
BARTON, David: former Chairman, Federal Trust for Education and Research, London
BIEHL, Dieter: Johan Wolfgang Goethe University, Frankfurt
BLUM, Peter: State Parliament of Lower Saxony, Hanover
BOGDANOR, Vernon: University of Oxford
BOISSERÉE, Klaus: Economic and Social Committee of the EC; City Counsellor, Düsseldorf
BRATT, Christian: Swedish Employers' Confederation, Stockholm
BRAUN, Albert: Kantonschule, Heerbrugg
CASPARIE, Ruurd: NATO Defence College, Rome

CORELL, Hans: Ministry of Foreign Affairs, Stockholm
DÄSTNER, Christian: State Chancellory, Nordrhein-Westfalen
DENTON, Geoffrey: Wilton Park
DE ZORDI, Guido: Kantonschule, St Gallen
DUSCHNER, Gabrielle: Department of National Defence, Ottawa
EKINS-DAUKES, Wilfred: Council of the European Communities, Brussels
ELLEFSEN, Harald: Conservative Member of the Norwegian Parliament
FENGER-MOELLER, Grethe: Conservative Member of the Danish Parliament
FERRILLO, Raphaël: Federal Administration of Finance, Bern
FORSYTH, Murray: Centre for Federal Studies, University of Leicester
FOSSUM, John: University of Bergen
GERBER-WIRZ, Christian: Kantonschule, St Gallen
GIUNTA, Giovanni: Federal Office of Foreign Economic Affairs, Bern
GRAHAM, Brenda: Raytown High School, Raytown, Missouri
GULBRANDSEN, Thor-Eirik: Labour Member of the Norweigan Parliament
GÜNTHARDT, Madeleine: Kantonschule Rämibühl, Zürich
HÄBERLIN, Ernst: Kantonschule, St Gallen
HENNET, Germain: Swiss Bankers' Association, Basel
HOVE, David: Kantonschule, Heerbrugg
JOST, Urs: Kantonschule, Zürich
KARRER, Mark: Gymnasium Rämibühl, Zürich
KAUFMANN-BÜHLER, Werner: Federal Ministry of Foreign Affairs, Bonn
KEEFE, Denis: Foreign and Commonwealth Office, London
KICKER, Renate: University of Graz
KRAEGE, Caroline: Federal Department of Foreign Affairs, Bern
KRETSCHMER, Friedrich: Federation of Germany Industry, Köln
KURER, Fred: Kantonschule, St Gallen
LATTER, Richard: Wilton Park
LEGG, Judy: Foreign and Commonwealth Office, London
LENK, Karin: Federal Ministry of Foreign Affairs, Wien
van LOOPIK, Adri: Ministry of Foreign Affairs, Den Haag
LYONS, John: Member, Wilton Park Academic Council

MELDGAARD, Anne-Marie: Social Democrat Member of the Danish Parliament

MICHALSKI, Anna: Royal Institute of International Affairs, Chatham House, London

MÜLLER, Karl Ulrich: Federal Ministry of Foreign Affairs, Bonn

NAEF, Walter: Kantonschule, St Gallen and University of Zürich

NEPF, Alfred: Federal Ministry of Finance, Wien

NEUNREITHER, Karlheinz: Secretariat of the European Parliament, Strasbourg

NIJENHUIS, Hinkinus: Ministry of Foreign Affairs, The Hague

OVERÅ, Oddvar: Deputy Secretary General, Norwegian Parliament

PINDER, John: College of Europe, Bruges

RICKENBACH, Peter: Kantonschule, St Gallen

RIEDEL, Arno: Federal Ministry of Foreign Affairs, Wien

SANGOLT HJORTLAND, Linda: University of Bergen

SCHEGG, Meinrad: Kantonschule, St Gallen

SCHELTER, Kurt: Bavarian State Ministry for Federal and European Affairs

SCHENKER, Ulrich: Kantonschule, Frauenfeld

SCHINDLER, Dietrich: University of Zürich

SCHMIDT, Helmut: Kantonschule, St Gallen

STAVA, Per: Norwegian School of Management, Sandvika

TESKE, Horst: Ministry of Justice, Bonn

TEUFEL, Gerhard: Management Academy of the State of Baden-Württemberg, Karlsruhe

TSCHIRF, Matthias: Federal Ministry for Federal Relations and Administrative Reform, Wien

VAN RHIJN, Arnold: Ministry of Economic Affairs, Den Haag

VOEGTLE, Otmar: Kantonschule, St Gallen

WALLACE, Helen: University of Sussex

WEIBEL, Paul: Kantonschule, St Gallen

WESTH, Bjoern: Social Democrat Member of the Danish Parliament

WISTRICH, Ernest: Former Director, UK Council of the European Movement

WOLF, Adam: Private Secretary to Prime Minister, Copenhagen

WOLF, Martin: *Financial Times,* London

WUERMELING, Joachim: Bavarian State Ministry for Federal and
   European Affairs
ZIEGLER, John: Hendrix College, Conway, Arkansas

Printed in the United Kingdom for HMSO
Dd295746 3/93 C6 G3397 10170